The
Real Enough
World

WESLEYAN POETRY

Also by Karen Brennan

Poetry

Here on Earth

Memoir

Being With Rachel

Fiction

Wild Desire

The Garden in Which I Walk

The
Real Enough World

KAREN BRENNAN

Wesleyan University Press | Middletown, Connecticut

Published by Wesleyan University Press, Middletown, CT 06459
www.wesleyan.edu/wespress
Printed in the United States of America
5 4 3 2 1

LIBRARY OF CONGRESS CATALOGING-IN-PUBLICATION DATA
Brennan, Karen, 1941–
  The real enough world / Karen Brennan.
    p. cm. — (Wesleyan poetry)
  ISBN-13: 978–0–8195–6751–2 (alk. paper)
  ISBN-10: 0–8195–6751–5 (alk. paper)
  ISBN-13: 978–0–8195–6752–9 (pbk. : alk. paper)
  ISBN-10: 0–8195–6752–3 (pbk. : alk. paper)
  I. Title. II. Series.
  PS3552.R378R43 2005
  811'.54—dc22   2005005620

For Tom Stillinger

CONTENTS

Acknowledgments

The author wishes to acknowledge the journals in which some of these poems first appeared: "Two Prose Poems" and "Tributes and Tribulations" in *Cue, a Journal of Prose Poetry*; "Four Ex Votos," "Sweat," "Sonora," "R," "Forgetfulness," "R," in *Interim*; "The Logic of Views" (part 2), "Rat Smith," and "Ear Surgean" in *Barrow Street*; "Picnic," "Hiddenness," Philosophy: A Play" in *Colorado Review*; "Likewise" in *Journal of the Southwest*; "Prayer for X" and "Prayer for Y" appeared in other forms in *Interim* and *Colorado Review*.

For friendship and encouragement during the writing of this manuscript, special thanks to Brian Blanchfield, Kate Coles, Peter Covino, Disa Gambera, Claudia Keelan, Jane Miller, Julie Paegle, Donald Revell, Stephen Romaniello, Nicole Walker, Gibb Windahl, and the late Aga Shahid Ali.

When I was a kid I was confined to a rock in the front yard.
Across the street other kids dared me to move.
I wore a pinafore from Saks, a barrette in my hair,
saw the world through my bangs, saw my bangs
looming before the world, like a hedge.
Little bird, little bird.
My tongue enraptured in my mouth.
My missing tooth spot.
Around the rock grew grass, but not anything special.
My shoes were patent leather.
My fingernails trimmed.
I cannot emphasize enough how clean I was kept
by my mother who sat sentry at the upstairs window
in her soft hairnet, with her sharp, worried nails,
calling down, *Don't you get dirty! Don't you cross
the street!* Oh I suppose I was happy enough.
Clouds came & went. Boys threw baseballs
which rolled into the gutter alongside our curb.
The neighbor girl climbed to the top of her apple
tree & waved. Once I saw her falling,
falling through limbs & unripe apples,
snapping off everything—the limbs, the apples—
& then she lay on the ground, a bruised sack,
crying & holding her knee.
The world was a dangerous place. Cars could come.
Wicked men wearing neckerchiefs could carry you off
in their hobo sacks. You might trip over
a log & break your neck & wind up in a coma.
Lightning could strike out your eye.
Little bird, little bird,
lightning would strike out your eye,
men would steal your brightest jewels,
but you were my darling future.

LITTLE BIRD

Dear little reader (I almost said
radar):
Take my wallet, credit cards
pearl necklace
cantilevered bra
high heels
my tongue & its wagging fits
my piercings
my toenail polish
                        You are welcome also to my underpants
the turquoise with sequined stars
the red with polka dots & worn-out elastic
& my momentarily opinionated world view
for what it's worth
& my cigarettes
& all the musings that match
my cigarettes
take my whole pocketbook full of kleenexes
& astrological forecasts—
a capricorn, I am prone to gloom anyway
& lucklessness in love & colds—
take my runny nose, therefore, & my sore throat
& the fog that clogs my sinuses
& the tree that shimmers in the fog
& the *stimmung* of grief with its sad limbs
& the leaves that waver & spill
into the deep, ghostly lake which I can hardly see
& my book of plans
on-hold & my various pleasures
crossed-out
                    Oh I am so hopeless
you could even shoot me, dear reader, but
you'll be wanting my scientific
theories & my future novel
& my future hat
whose ribbons are recitals
whose flowers are applause

I saw the bellman swinging a chicken that looked like a cat—
I saw the bellman eating steak—
I saw the bellman weeping, leading a woman into a hole—
I saw the bellman encumbered with luggage, shrieking, clawing at a door—
I saw the bellman walking around calmly
then setting the table
then pulling out his wallet—
Things were good for the bellman until the monster came—
Things were fine until his wife left him for a sailor or an ape—
for an investment banker with a cape—
Things were AOK until he fainted under the green awning
Then he got a hair cut, which I also saw
& a tooth pulled
& a beautiful new set of brass pantaloons
& a raise—
& then the screen went blank—
Opulent darkness filled the theater
& I didn't know where to look.

EAR SURGEON

The ear surgeon needs an ear if he is to ply his trade.
He needs the hammer, anvil, stirrup.
He needs the drum and possibly drum sticks
for snacks, but very little, minuscule & a tiny scalpel &
an infection. If he is beautiful he must empty
himself of beauty, whoosh. & whoosh for all
heartache & likewise for philosophical thinking
which he is prone to
being an ear surgeon & he must be able in a blink
to shrink himself to squeeze through caverns
plugged with boredom & heartache
for which he also needs a pick &
goggles & a tape recorder.
He will be in there for a long long long time.
He will record moans so sweet to his own ear
he will have erections
& a deafening thrum thrumming & another noise
like a creek gurgling up & another
like an egg frying &
a few more that are only lost metaphors, half
of what he heard . . .
He is the ear surgeon of the 21st century.
He will untune himself &
whisper deep into his own waxes.
The ear surgeon, my only hope.

In a tall building
on a city street, in a corner of a restaurant
where a girl is ordering spaghetti
& a man touches her arm
& the waiter rubs his eye on his apron
in the fold of the apron
in the purple shadow, there
in a smudge, a thing undefinable
hard to see, or in the eye itself,
the antipasto olive which
has a shine & a pit—
however, the girl is so bored
wearing a scarf
fiddling with fringes
(in the weave of the scarf, in the tines of the fringes
& the man is wearing a cheap green sweater
(in the fur of his conversation
(in the teeth of her thoughts
in the shifty moment
in the criss-crossed light
in the scuttle of vowels
in her beige yawn
as it spools from her beige mouth.
O maker of all things!

O now the die has been
cast upon swine & pearls,
he mused, have little hints of yellow
which nullify.
B was his first idea
rising in a plume
B for Bombs & pies
like the Boysen & the Black
over which a mountain outline
seemed too mere, too shallow
upon the cloud-shaped
bear. At any rate, a wand
was involved & lots of
grimy wind & a pencil &
an eye-shade.   Then he wept
& his handkerchief streamed from his pocket
in a fine sail.

I took the donkey for a walk—
we saw the ceramic city
the paving stones of ice
the terrible wind with its puffed, sarcastic cheeks.
Down by the sea we saw kids sunbathing
& mothers in bikinis
& a few men jerking off on the side wall.
We saw a little boat far out in the distance
jolting along, but precariously,
& we were worried.
We turned from this scene.
We had taken all the pleasure we could
& we were tired.
On the way home we met a man in a slicker
who said how much for the mule?
He looked the way you'd expect: yellow beard hairs,
eye-beads in a nest of furrows
& folded newspapers. Within this face, I thought, is another
original face. So I sold him the donkey
&
that night I missed the donkey.
Then I regretted everything:
the white sheets, my clothes in a lump on the floor,
the bodies of stars & their refusal to speak sense
& even you I regretted.
I'll say it again: I even regretted you.

No wooden doll involved
no automaton
no fireplace coals glowing like eyes
nor a spectacle salesman
called Coppola
who is the double of an evil lawyer
called Coppelius.
No doubles
evil or otherwise.
No suicide at the end.
No love story either
no thwarted love
no love supreme.
Therefore, no love props—
flowers, rings, gifts of tea
stolen bracelets with green stones
which the heroine nevertheless accepts
because it strikes her as sweet
as well as deplorable—the theft,
the gift of the theft.
In fact, there is an absence
of female characters, so
the heroine is not involved
she with her stolen bracelet,
with her tea
nor is Coppola or Coppelius
—whatever his name is—
with his pocket perspective
used for spying on Olimpia
who is an automaton,
& who may in her woodenness
resemble the heroine
but who appears nowhere.
While in the background
behind a rather ornate gold-colored grate
the coals do not smolder
therefore they are not symbols.
There are no symbols

no uncanny reappearances
no bitter break-up or sad aftermath
or over-determined keepsakes—
as, for example, the bracelet of the heroine
would have been, had the heroine
been involved
which she wasn't.
Sometimes she wonders if she ever was.

BABY BLUES

Cruising down the highway
in his white Dodge pick-up
the baby's on his way to score.
        uh huh, uh huh   ·
On his way to score.
        oh yeah.
Wonder if the man'll be waiting
where he said he'd be.
        uh huh
Where he said he'd be
in the Ford Taurus over by the hill.
The baby's got twenty bucks
& no luck.
        uh huh, uh huh
Oh the baby
whose mama is but a thin
dream of a mama.
Even to herself a thin dream
cropping up
in these rooms like any old envelope
the bills come in
waiting for the trash.
Waiting for the trash, uh-huh.
In these rooms where the baby unpleasantly
paces, crying
I'm so lonely, I'm so sad, I'm so empty
        oh yeah.
The ceiling is falling down
& we're both pinned beneath
& I can't catch my breath.
Honestly mom, I can't catch my breath.

My sleeve catches fire.
Madame's hairbrush is spotted in a nest of spiders.
The bread, stale, moldy,
the curtain rods askew.
I am shivering in a thin polka-dotted apron.
My master has gone to murder a man with a club-foot.
The eggs are overdone,
therefore inedible,
therefore beasts, yoked beasts
& my breast heaves mountainous sighs
for one so small at the rib.
Please pay all the bills right now!
I cannot stand anymore these interruptions!
The lady of the house collapses at the bannister.
The air has little jagged spikes.
The slanted shadows on a neighboring lawn
brook a thousand anthills,
no *ressentiment*
no flocked sparrows tuning their cutlery
or whacking their feathers like fans
& meanwhile the newspaper still in folds at the foot of the porch steps
meekly bristles
as do the whiskers of the cat.

Here dawn curls around a tiny painted village, mingles with factory smoke. Virgin's cape of stars, two brothers or an in-law wearing an open collar, hospital bed at such odd perspective, posed & inhabited, coordinates of black railings, paper flowers. If the body is awake, if the body is dreaming, if the body is on the mend. These words, healing in its moment of dissolve. The cup on the nightstand, the window with its flap of gray drape, the bowl of fruit, the eyelids' flutter, grace of floorboards and yellow, brood of prayers which one might bring forth, a chicken dinner (bones at best) or a little gold bracelet adorned with sapphires, take everything.

Thank me for this. The window from which you make your escape is unguarded. The deity is off-duty, down with the plague. The striped Guatemalan bedspread, the lumpy, undreamable pillows, the blue painted table with its stacks of bad literature & rolling papers, the cathedral bells gong-gong-gonging any old time, the parade's trumpet & drum as clear as if it were Billie singing East of the Sun, & all my happiness, thousands of rose bouquets that pummeled me, instead of.

Stupid stupid. Bird screech saying I do not love either you or you. Washing dishes or declaiming that to be declaimed in bravery or otherwise. The night you threw the dinner plate against the wall, screamed for hours my name. Lovemaking as arguments. Then music, then tears, then slamming the door & you saying you always leave & me, o the pure drama, o the uncalled for exquisite drama, poor us. On another planet we split things up—the wheat, the wine, the bed, & it went on forever in the divides where things sluiced inward, where things rolled over. Star star. Do not forget anything, not a word.

A word whose map is red. Is indelible. Who are the bad neighbors, those party girls who fuck deep into morning coffee, bang the walls like horses? This is a paper den, fragile shuddering house where chairs leap up, cups hold shaky, moldering futures. I thought it was ordained, even pre-ordained. My clothes all over the place, green scarf on chair, pink on bed, shirt across your back, hurled. Libidinal unfold, then boredom. Then beyond in the green limbs, everything stays green.

The swallows were riding the swell, the swell leapt. I the nameless kept my heart in my purse. I was nobody's true love, at the moment, & so I scanned the arena looking for a number of qualities. Heavens, there were so many rocks, so much water rushing in between! A flossy cottonwood dazzled into the speedy surface & my palms actually tingled. I still wanted adventure, after all these years, & it was beginning to wear thin. Thin also the clouds, the planets, the photograph of mom & pop on my kitchen table, the dog-eared magazines, the bowl of peaches, the straw rug, the fireplace decor, the postcard from X, the dryer lint with its little blue worlds, the stove grit & anger, the refrigerator slime oozing toward the tv chair already chocolate-smeared, the show about rhinos, the phone call from X, the show about dating, the show about emergency surgery, the lace curtain, the window ledge with its silver layer of dust, the view. All this way for nothing.

TWO PROSE POEMS

1

Reading from her critically acclaimed blah blah, Blah Blah will once again grace us with her presence, etc blah blah blah. The library will serve in a fishbowl everything you thought you'd read. Once upon a time, though, even the fish were bored. Traffic: too much of it. Then, chicken wings & a kind of harrowing experience with a cab. She wore what you'd expect with a name like that. Standing on the podium instead of "at," residing in her own wavering simulacra on the wall. Also on the wall little shadows of turnips & gloves. & at the opera a wail comes out of nowhere & the walrus still has that walk. You know the walk.

2

Her name was F but everyone called her Y. In the museum the boys had other plans. The hallway was dark and a little frighteningly cold, so that my arm kept going limp. Jack said, Over here, haul it over here. Dick said, I can't seem to get a good grip on the edges. A rectangle of sky. A triangle of roof. What means these views? Where has the hope gone, the feeling of hilarity we briefly encountered like a row of little bleeding ants? The end of the end is frequently like this, reams of beauty like smoke unfurling, then hair, then inciting some crazy movement in a tunnel. We have to keep doing what we're doing, she whispered. Or else we'll all die sooner than we thought.

For dinner a snack of sausages, broccoli on the side. A disagreement on
the side & roses as a first course. The plant needs watering as the entre &
then for dessert a dirty joke which begins like this a traveling salesman
went to a farmhouse which was followed by a nice sauterne, apples, wedge
of blue cheese. All the guests were delighted. My carafe runneth full &
blind. My roses were themselves, repeatedly perfectly.

As an afterthought, the backyard held some greenery. Spectacular chest-
nuts were placed under the tongue. The boy, who had ridden his bicycle
to the edge of the Sound expressed himself crudely, but I loved his hands
& the grubby knuckles as if a cloud could punch. I loved his tearing at the
knee and shrieking, a voice caught between oaks. Like milk rushing into
a jar that formerly held roses, I was gearing up to recover the trees of my
childhood. & the leaves melted, they tuned out. As did the landscape's
shadow, the miraculous birds, the soft weeping inconsolable willow.

We arrive with expectation & leave with hats, not ours. A whisper along
the tracks of floor boards, creak of galoshes, as in the story where snow
falls as a metaphor, covers our heads & scarves. Made tender. Made
nervous, as we two squinting up faces. Cannot see the road as when, in a
careworn instant, a small unidentifiable sound may suddenly strike us as
possessing mystery.
     In this way we make a chain linked fence.   Or a mood   Or a tunnel.

SELF-PORTRAITIST IN TWO MOODS

Two fruits, lemon & apple.
A silver cave, as of a shadow.
A blue hat, as of a halo.
Many serendipitous brushes
for the life inside the pupil &
oh yes, a tea-set, chairs & linens,
the artist's self-annihilating
vanity, seen in the downward
-casting mouth, a looming head
& flat brown hair—
burnt umber unmixed.

*

Just as a dog or two leaps up
to snatch a bone from
who? a pal
& races wherever he races
& is generally happy
so too, I am not
at all aimless these days
nor is the ant a good metaphor
for she is never not a part
of her swarming shadow going
dutifully into a hole.
Not these,
but not not these either.

love-struck, she decided to keep it at bay. This was the time of her life. The beds were nicely arranged & the pillows—oh the pillows. (Too many pillows her last ex-husband had said, too much fluff everywhere daunting my best propositions.) Undaunted, she persisted: lipstick, eyeliner. But memory intervened with its knuckles. Blood flew or flowed. Nightgown in tatters & the bathroom door now sported a hole the size of Mexico. Through which little sparrows zoomed & paper flowers, petal by petal, cascaded to the hall floor, as if someone had grown weary of this & all ritual. No notes in bottles, no appetizers, no sex. At this point we leave her. At this point, she is getting dimmer.

years later she noticed the sun in its socket. The neighbor was playing his guitar. Everything appeared to be marvelous. She purchased another pair of high heels & lit a cigarette. She cooked a bouillabaisse, stitched a stocking, telephoned her broker. It was winter so soon & beneath her porch came the cry of newborn kittens, so felicitous in a poem. Then spring came gushing in, the melt akin to familiar, akin to loss. Evaporation continued in her life, dance floors wobbled, petunias sprung up & she among them, a little flimsy.

full circle & she's dating a dull man. She goes to a shrink, confesses her abundancies, including pillows—oh the pillows. Nature has turned bitter & unforgiving. Repetition makes her nervous. She is old now, tired of the porch & the mail. The kittens, now beasts, are spiritless, quarrelsome. But memory intervenes with its skies. The dull man puts on a cape & saws her in half. One half creeps to the window, cocks its luckless ear. A voice comes from somewhere—she knows its slow pivots, fiery angles, its sharp spokes of indifference, but she can't place it.

Spider City

After a while I dreamt about
    the Spider City
& when I woke up in my
    flannel pj's
the curtain flapped open
    & the sky greeted me.

Hello Karen, Hello Little Bee,
    it said which is when
I remembered the strange
    webbed sky of the Spider
City & your face in the
    middle saying Kiss Me.

Breathless City

Every city is a little breathless,
a little behind the times,
racing to catch up, thus
gasping.

That day I wore a gray suit,
    white gloves, 1960 or so.
Some thin man approached
    & offered me $$ to
    pose in the nude.
The sun over St. Patrick's
    Cathedral like a child's
sun, all rays around
    a smiling face
& the man whose gray suit
    matched my own was
    called Ray!

    Such coincidences
occur in a city whose heart

splits open in two shocks.
But this happened later.
& I wasn't around
though I watched it on TV.

Dapper City

In Florida the palm branches
    rustle like neckties,
the ocean a gilded
    cologne we plunder,
the grass, green as the
    stolen eye of the Dowager
or a bruised infant
which is so sad
found in the trash can
among some white receipts
& spaghetti.
              I am smoking a cigarette
wishing it were over—
the parasols, the gliding waterway
    ships, the cocktails,
the aces & clubs, the languorous beach
    stretches, the strings of pearls,
hats—
wishing it would begin again.

Dieting City

Or Starving City. It's hard
    to tell. For one thing, it's
    dark & for another
    I feel inadequate.
My perpetual motion has
    ceased to amuse anyone here
    (I confide) even though . . .

I wore a beautiful skirt of red silk
    & when I whirled you could

see everything—
the river
with its captured lights, the
glint of bridges, the
pock-marked Palisades,
aflame.

So much of this is untrue.

A worm slunk in the sidewalk cracks.
An old, old woman, wreathed
        in snot,
spoke sharply: She said,
"just because you give me five dollars
don't entitle you to my life's story."

City of Jokes

A man goes to a psychiatrist
        sporting a huge gash in his
        forehead, says I bit
        myself. How did you
        do that? asks the psychiatrist.
        It was easy, says the man.
        I stood on a stool.
Afterwards, I pulled out of
        the parking garage & the
        day was overcast, streets
        icy.
I drove up the hill & took
        a right. I drove by the
        drive-in coffee place &
        the brown house with the
        shutters & took a left
        & then I was home.
        I turned
on the radio at this point.
A girl with a cane made her way
        down the sidewalk.
She was a stranger,
& she was my daughter.

Elizabethan City

I encountered Hamlet in a glade
& this scene, forsooth, changed into
hills &
then again a dark chamber
in which my own mother lay dying.

I wish it were another era
        but things occur where
        they will
& my defenses are poor ones.

        She has elegant bones which,
in age, have become sharp &
unfriendly.

        (Oh the body weeps & slickers
of hair cover all of us who
keep vigils.)

In a moment, I too, would
        invent a soliloquy about
        existence.

My heart in its jeweled box
        as of nothing
& zero the shape of
sorrow which doesn't
add up.

City of Dot Dot Dot

There was a window, a drape,
        a venetian blind thickened with
        dust, an accordion sound
up from the street . . .
Your friend the author [was] inside
this which was inside that which was

once again . . .
ad nauseum . . .
contained in . . .
etc etc . . .
   Space
   shrinks & even afternoons
   which once seemed so voluminous
   have dwindled to a sad heap . . .
Little wrinkled days no longer
   unfold . . . Lawns have grown
minuscule & purposeless . . . Hairs
sprout on the female chin & buildings
formerly majestic are . . .
But I was crazy then . . .
In the fullness of each moment . . .
I walked everywhere in the gloam & sand . . .

City of Basements

Of course, conducive to sleep.
Of course, musty & poorly
   organized. You wouldn't go there
   uninvited. I wouldn't invite you.
But there are chinks in the brick ceilings
   that make it seem radiant
elsewhere, which is a blessing.

& amid the rats & spider houses
I might invent something
spectacular (I almost believe).

This is all I have to say about it.
Because it is unamenable to description.
Because even now my eyes are closing.

Pity yourself, Sister.
Life is harder than you dreamed possible.

WHEREFORE HERE WITH THEE

PRAYER FOR X

the green world

a preference for green

in the light a filament

reminds me of love

shapes & natures

traffic from a bridge

buildings mournful

cracked remedy

listening landscape

culled from my ankle

culled from my shoe

oh nowhere is where

oh nowhere is where

poor me sings the mother

awake in her nightgown

unfolding her glasses

unoccupied cavern

a sea with a mouth

it's me sings the cup

it's just me sings the saucer

me too sings the world

the word   the wall

the worry   the worm

the wreck   the wing

the west   the way

the wrangler   the writer

the wrestler   the wren

the wild   the while

R. says: I'm not by nature a depressed person.
I have a right to know.
I have a right to know

what I put into my body.
No anti-depressants. Why didn't I die?
Why didn't I just die?

On the other hand, this is a challenge.
Do you think it is a challenge?
Have I?

I wanted to die
& didn't remember.
Only a vague vagueness

like a color you never heard of.
The popping-in-place rain.
Think of drops like that.

When I was a kid
I saw it all up close; the box
of Cheerios

& on every living room window
a separate river.
Thus trees & cars shimmered

& my own blue eyes
were invisible.
In a coma

I sweated bullets
according to my mother.
Quarts of water, weeks on end.

This was in the interim care unit in Bountiful.
She wrung one washcloth after
another.

Bountiful (as a place-name) gives me the creeps.
I never opened my eyes.
Why didn't I die then?

My face so pale & pointless like a little wet bird.
Meaning I didn't flinch.
Not when they suctioned my trach,

not when they pulled my hair
or stuck me full of Heparin in the stomach
so I wouldn't develop clots.

Nothing meant anything.
I could have been dead or flying
out of myself

for all I knew or still know
since my memory is shot & even my dreams
evaporate quicker than most.

Even the smells of my dreams.
She wrung one washcloth after another
into a plastic basin

until there was a little pool of my sweat
in there
splashing around.

She said she had to call the nurse
for more wash cloths
& then, by accident, she discovered the linen room

—fresh, white towels piled to the ceiling
—the heavenly smell of bleach
She buried her face in a warm towel

thinking, *it's so fucked up.*
Nearby the parents of kids folding laundry.
And the boy Luke

left for dead in a park at nine months
capable only of a squealing noise & the boy with the birthday cake
wandering the corridors in a helmet

& Lucy with her respirator & Carlos
who drools in front of television.
Meanwhile I sweated out my whole life. Past & future

beaded up on my forehead,
pored from my pores.
Oh life

she wondered,
my mother who sopped it up.

Today I read about the territorial
great purple hairstreak,
wood rats,

horned lizards, Gambel's quail,
black-tailed jackrabbits,
myriad washes,

rocky outcrops.
Phrases like minimal rainfall,
like withered

agave stump
made me feel a little off balance,
as if the world were reading my mind,

wave upon wave.
In the distance heat creates a ripple
which turns the air to water.

The stigmata have reappeared on my forearm:
A crop of blood red splotches
whose correspondence to cactus flowers

scares me.
But I'm not dying any more than
jojoba seeds, harvest beetles, flies, bees'

stiletto beaks poised to pierce a pollinator
are dying. Not death
but a kind of cool, rectangular

emptying out.
The glint of Rachel's four-pronged cane,
some rhythmic tapping—

rain? her shoes?—
the crab spider's near perfect
yellow camouflage

her cane weaving between leaves & weeds,
the glint of stone walls (the stones
all colors, beige, orange, mauve

violet). Our uncertain boundaries.
Sometimes my hand through my hair feels like her hand,
the way, as she slowly came to life

she would reach out
& run her fingers through. & now
I feel the past is in a cloud

& memories are little chinks of
color drifting by,
seen peripherally, like dust or shadow

or some unnatural afterimage printed
on the retina,
almost ironic & continually

vanishing.
My head is light, as in light-headed
& dizzy with forgetting.

Things spin on the ground.
The orange flower with its tiny slippered cup
I carelessly tromp,

as though blind.
The desert shimmers up ahead & who knows
what violence occurs or

how the present lizard is
obliterated each moment, with or
without us. Meanwhile

The feel of my shoes,
sunglasses.
A girl's shiny, apocryphal, black blouse.

She walks with a limp, as do I.
Inside we are always weeping or laughing.
I'd like to think the landscape means something—

the vast sky
the gray, big-fisted saguaros
the arroyo with its astonishing name—

but it doesn't.

R

Once I dreamt everything that wound up happening.
Hard to believe
but it was all there—the accident, the wheelchair,

everything. The nurse with the fat face & the palest
flyaway hair. The doctor who said
aphasia and made us cry,

who scrutinized my face as if I were some curious
recipe or swatch of fabric—
Others whose hands were rough or soft or tedious or cold or misguided,

who smelled of cigarettes or cream or fruited gum or cafeteria
spaghetti or medicine.
I never loved any of them—even when their hair

slipped from their little hats
or when I saw in their lying down eyes something approaching
tenderness.

I knew every one of them in my dream,
their hairdos, uniforms.
In my room a window looked out on a wall.

Snow against brick. How amazing! I thought in my dream.
My sheets scratchy on my legs.
I couldn't walk.

I couldn't eat or speak or think
very well.
I saw my mother in a cloud. Her face would grow

& shrink. Grow & shrink & make this clicking
sound, as if she were slowly
unraveling

like a film shown backwards
or like a telescope revolving against the planetary sky.
Against the planetary sky of glowless stars

& constellations spinning dumbly. That's how she struck me.
I couldn't help it.
I believe she dreamt me into being in my dream.

But who knows how the dream predicts a mother's twirling face
or how with her ministering fingers
she must have held my hand?

I myself have no memory.
That is to say, my points a & b are disconnected
as in a game unsolved.

Snow against brick. Amazingly ugly.
The dull flakes filling the window so that I start to
ache in my wrists

wanting, I suppose, to reach out.

FORGETFULNESS

The sky is vast.
The white buildings so clean-lined
along the streets.

Rachel loves Mexico.
The waiters give her *limonade*
& tapes.

Sylvio Rodriguez, Caballo Dorado,
but we forgot the walkman.
We forgot the walkman,

I tell her.
The sky is navy blue at dawn
against the orange wall

then gradually lightens
in swirls, like cream dissolved in coffee.
Where is my walkman?

Rachel asks.
Perseveration. Forgetfulness.
Simon Bolivar, she tells Arturo. *Raquel,* he calls her.

The sky awash with breezes.
Palm leaves sharp as crops of rustling swords.
Clouds like wooden blocks.

The sky contains us like a milky moon.
A glassy fetaled egg.
A metal boat.

At sunset there are pink rivers.
Minuscule explosions of green atomic light
scrape the surface of my skin.

A gray hand spreads its gray fingers.
It's true, I told the shrink, this feeling of tears
overcomes me.

Daily overcomes me.
Everything so beautiful in the world,
seductive,

one wants to dive in, I tell him.
Wasn't Lethe a river? I mean I understand the
impulse.

To be elsewhere? he says. Yes, I say.
That & to speak adoringly, to find the words that match
this view . . .

Likewise, my daughter says this mood washes
over her. Unexpected.
She refuses medication. Sobs. I see her sweet features crumble.

Everything is so difficult.
I used to be a runner.
She is standing at the mirror in her underwear.

Her right hand clenched at her side.
Holding onto the sink, then the wall,
she makes her way to her chair.

Her lipstick is crooked.
Her face when she's sad looks
covered up.

Features cramped.
As if trying to squeeze into a smaller space.
Sweetheart

I say. Her smile flares like a match.
The shocked color of hibiscus
or bougainvillea

suddenly there.
I love you.
When she began to awaken

her eyelid cracked open, a blue chink
like glass.
Just one eyelid—her left—

blue glass like the blue flowers on the vine
entangled in the Queen's palm
or like a swimming pool with its various lights

& fractured depths,
that left eye followed me
from the window to the door to the

side of her bed.
I used to put my head on her pillow
& stare into her skin.

R

I am watching her from a height. I try
to explain this.
She is skewed a little to the left. And lower.

I'm a girl with no memory. Or rather
it comes in spurts: *non ricordi nieto.* Like that.
Also the Arno

the color of bones & laundry & beasts
from some old book of mine.
Also running along somewhere up a mountain

which I loved—
both the mountain & the running.
If I could lose my breath, dear God, let it be now,

I used to think. Because it was glorious.
You felt the clouds race into your lungs & you knew
we were all composed of everything:

Not only blood but grass; not only skin but layers
of flaked time.
Therefore, somewhere is my lost memory.

Among the dizzy leaves of cottonwood
or sticking to a rock
like "where's Waldo,"

waiting to be spotted.
This in my heart I know. Though I can't prove it.
I lack the proof

as some can be said to lack courage
or feeling.
This is my problem.

My mother is my memory, I tell her,
down among the brambles
if you'll excuse the cliché, if this is a cliché.

I remember the future. The future snow &
future gorgeous light around
the car—

I remember being lifted up.
I hardly spoke.
I said my prayers each night.

I walked with a cane
& hung my head a little as I stepped
each step.

FAITH

Contemplating the light painted on leaves,
the outlines & vortecii & cups of leaves
filled or drenched with light

leaves the length of a foot
positioned vertically
behind which a two-year-old pushes his own stroller.

R drinking juice
saying, when the spirit moves you, let it groove you
how groovy are breakfasts in Mexico?

How groovy I ask you?
This morning I knelt on the stone floor
& prayed.

Enough is enough, I said,
talking tough to God. I've had it
I said.

Then I waited for a miracle,
any sign, like a glass of water tipping
or the door

suddenly swinging open.
Nothing.
But it could have been anything—

the sound of the wind
dying down so that a purer nothing
came along—

or if I were to yawn or my eyelids
unexpectedly flutter.
I'd accept anything.

Yesterday we met Manuel, paralyzed for nine years
who lives in a house with no doors,
lies on a canvas cot, makes purses from little

rectangular pieces of paper.
I bought one for R who thinks it's funky.
Last night my dreams

over-dramatized,
like a painting by Caravaggio.
A woman I used to know drowned in a pool.

Then I awoke to the silver sound
of the filter,
two yellow tubes afloat, smacking the edges.

Mexican orange honeysuckle snoozing on vines. The sky
smeared half-white.
I am thinking of Manuel's feet like dead fish

encased in dirty white socks.
His catheter bag hanging by his side,
his very pale pee,

the fly he brushed from his arm,
his chipped front tooth. For two years
he lay on the cot,

listened to the sounds of cars outside
& an old radio. Sylvia who tends him is fierce,
some fanatical mood in her face. I know this mood.

Mira, she says, It's a miracle.
Instead we see
walls the same color as the socks as

today's sky. Nail holes &
the patched marks of old tape & one current
calendar with a Toreador, a bull snorting

into a cape.
On the mantle some bright orange plastic clock
& from the corner of my eye I spot the kitchen's

linoleum table & a row of filled
jars.
Sylvia holds the rosary to Rachel.

Mija, she says. I will pray for you. She says it slowly,
in English.
She is drained by the power of faith,

she tells me.
I see it draining her like the angel in Caravaggio's
painting holding back the dangerous arm

of Jacob, whose faith was perfect.
In Sylvia's eyes everything, filling & emptying
like the sky

with stars, darkness
& now a kind of bleached blue
behind enormous fig trees.

The woman face down
sinking slowly through layers of blue
swimming pool water

wearing a black bathing suit.
I want to see the world beyond this one,
the arc of heaven,

my child singing today, walking
with her cane—
Hola que tal?—

The future of her past self—
the last lap of the 1500
& she's out front—

not so much fast as unstoppable—
green gym shorts,
freckles . . .

how one heart devolves on another.
The shrink says to me
I keep thinking *you* didn't get on that motorcycle.

but my hand through my hair
felt like her hand
& I remember how as an infant

she was covered with blond fur.
Is she there?
Is anyone there?

In the background she is laughing
her beautiful laugh.

trees & shadows

trees & shadows

expanding longly

coat & hat

away we go

the glove is gone

a sock of blue

& here's the shoe

the bed is white

the window burning

the sky a hum

the hum a wounded sound

dear dear dear sir

forgive the madness

bluest blank block

rock my rock

with thee in blankness rock

wherefore here with thee

THE PATH WE ARE ON

INVOCATION

It was morning & the soul

had wings. I counted four

   cactus wrens on the railing.

The road, which as you know, goes

  Up through the mesa, the pale

     green shrubs—creosote?—

formed a little s-shaped loop. I felt like dying.

  It was the moment itself.

    A blue mountain sloping

downward.

It was at the threshold of a world such as this that I stood in peril . . .
—Saint Augustine

1

                      To solve
    the problem which concerns
the question of yearning; of who yearns
       & wearing what hat, expressing what resolve

toward itself, like a star, hooded in light
       revolves toward you & me, standing
incredibly still, expanding
       that is, still expanding, as we might

compose or be seen as composing ourselves
       for heartache or otherwise.
          Consider the slow rise
       of the subject into image: a swell

of shade swinging somberly in place, so fragile
       we think it could be us, years from
now, holding our breaths, stunned
       out of self-reflection. You could say meanwhile

it all comes full circle. That is,
       the everyday paragraphs conclude at least
as gracefully as Caravaggio's shadows, a fleece
       of greying mauves surrounding the head of this

or that angel. Speaking of which desire
       always shades slant-wise, away from clarification
& into the blanker smudges which like vacation-
       ing lovers are labeled background or quagmire

or incidental to the scene of kissing: his arms
       criss-crossing her back like a bathing suit
her hair swimming on his shoulder; thoughts, in pursuit
       of which she stops to watch a swarm

of sand flies, like soot foreshadowing the ruin
    of everything, whoosh up. Oh no!
she thinks, but thinking it is not enough to slow
    the moment down, for soon

he'll leave, she knows, holding him there, against
    the blue and white geography, the crashing
inattentive waves and sand flies smashing
    into the wind like hope. The faintest

memory—this one—is not enough to store
    your words beneath us; like the tide's rough
ancillary thrust backwards, or the other stuff
    we left there—towels, oil—on the shore.

2

Back to Caravaggio. Stashing those
    chunks of darkness, the artful language of
drapery and armpit, Abraham above
    Isaac, the knife above Caravaggio's

version of the boy's face, terrified
    above the shadow of the rock, above the rock
itself, and in the background a city all flocked
    blue and gold, cypress and temple, like Paradise—

And so on. Truthfully I get tired of describing
    to myself—or you—how it might have happened or
whether it did and under what conditions I might be more
    receptive (why should I?). Not only one of us sliding

out of view, past the angel's yellow arm and the pointed
    finger, so unaccusatory, more like a gesture in dance
held too long. And this city, at a glance
    which happens to be mine is casually anointed

with little lights under an invisible horizon. Because
    after a certain time, in certain seasons, it is all

night, without fluctuation. And to think this fall
        from passion or grace conceived as pause

between objects or verbs or the cool drift of leaves
        speckling the canyon at dawn, the spare
and utter unconnectedness of leaves. And there
        you are, framed in the view-finder, you, griev-

ing for nothing. At best, a Kleenex, dropped
        and floating in the currents of my attention. Or your
attention. Perishable. Sacrifice equals love or
        does it merely equal loss, nothing beyond the stopped

life of itself. *Achoo*! Still one longs to write about
        stars these days or I do because they lift
a person up. But where to? A shift
        in focus shrinks or seems to shrink the eye, whereas a bout

of Beijing flu could be productive: Shivering in
        the tub, calling Mom, spilling the jar of Tylenol
on the white tiles. All these happy banal
        facts bolt us to the bed. Think of it: Caravaggio's hero

poised between the angel and the son, concentrating
        on the details. He'll get it right. It was always meant
to be art, not life. Not process or flux. I almost sent
        you a letter, a photograph, a poem, a painting.

I almost sent you a wall of skin, an arched spur
        from my deepest heart. That was when I wanted you.
I almost wanted you again. But time went and went on. So
        too everything—words & light & unaccountable pleasure.

3

She sleeps poorly, in these graceless
        covers, blue and white sheets, her old flat
down pillow crunched under, the quilt that
        used to be shared, now as if mindless

of her own life. The little green cornices
        of cozy sleep not creeping up
because she doesn't deserve it (rup-
        tured by the body's sweat). And old caresses

keep coming back in dreams. His knuckles
        or the way his jaw curves in a shadowy
line, back from the chin, his pale eyes
        closed. I wanted to swim in the reckless

centers, their apple. But some star-
        crossed wind prevailed; the world's
vague photographs swirled
        around my head, like sin or dust, marred

by nothing but the view itself
        bouncing continually back. As if any sphere
were enough to keep us rooted here
        to each other. As if you held

me continually, without regret. As if
        we were perfect & the light unending
& the bird's straight flight plunging
        us not into bottomless grief

but innocence for the last time. Seeming-
        ly eternal. A nexus of dry
branches where they land with a sigh
        fifteen feet above earth, dreaming

of nothing but repetition. Not dark
        elsewheres. Not the motel in Flagstaff
where you cut your hair & rebuffed
        me. Later the famous park

would freeze this recollection in vast
        otherworldly permanence—so
like desire with its purples & blues
        & solid cavernous edges & rust

& erosion. Here the deep rise of earth,
      here the spectacular web of eons
circling it unevenly. And now bands
      of something akin to light's stark

isness. Her long hair to match her face.
      His opening ploy. Her response.
His telling about it years later "and the dance
      was best of all," though she'd erase

the last part, where beneath his white shirt
      she felt his muscles tense and draw
back. A snarl of the body, whose aw-
      ful symmetry is hurt

in certain gut-level situations. Like when
      I used to ride my bike past all
those forsythia and pull
      them off one-handed—a thousand

little yellow stars on the sidewalk
      where more than once I broke my
mother's back. And then it was over suddenly,
      the bare limb rebuked me as my own unfinished thought

—the mother's back intact, the branch still green—
      wavered in my handlebars. But I steered straight
down Oak and onto Larch and envisioned my great
      future. This is it. I only seem

distressed. Beyond the wilderness
      of sorrow, whose meek embankments slug it out
with stones, & the falling, beautiful
      aforementioned leaves, is what? Is—?

PICNIC

What you fail to notice flashes

—fist of roses, cringe of grass—

That green

Having been freshly mowed

Having tasted like onions

Two little girls, to take an example,

The trees under which they sit forever

Birds' hands, mouth of iris, stipple

Of bench, hard-colored, dreamy nonetheless

If this life is a dream

& two girls in their pretty white dresses

Dark eyes gazing

But whatever that was is lost

We don't remember it

& this sky, the wrong

Color for itself

Not awash in anything

Not really *present* in the sense of

Chairs

The unemphatic present

Clusters of involved, inelegant sentences

Clusters of ants & whatever reverses that solitude

The slanted rain & dull thunderclap & grass all tamped down

Gleam of rod or sky

Some sky you might remember

The smell of lilacs coming back in monuments

The man mowing his lawn

Driving a van

Crouched beneath huge leaves

Your invisible eye of beholder

The bird in its wet nest

The child in her daze

Be not be preoccupied with looking. Go to the object; let it come to you.
—Henry David Thoreau

leaves
still mumbling on the hushed porch

~

                        "habit of attention"
                        eye of beholder
                        thigh of couch

~

fast microwavable current like blindness
traveling
spire of mouth

~

                        wanting you, not wanting you
                        wanting you, not wanting you
                        off-white sky

~

planes: lateral wood, vertical column, peak of
loquat, fat fuzzy leaves
displayed spread legs, cunt, etc.

~

motorcycle helmet under creosote

                        nothing but edges
                        split envelopes
                        arrival

~

Thoreau's journals
the eyes' facts
as the path veers off
I imagine coming closer   blinking or not

~

toward a state of relaxation
work with the pain as if
stewing vegetables

~

                    not just flowers & leaves
                    iris voluptuary clattering

alive
but the world's dense shadow hands
unfailingly held

~

beneath lichen & organism
bug's languid creep up
from clamor

~

                    saxophone & swimming pool
                    afternoon equaling this
                    beige dog in green ivy

~

like thought
spreading across a lawn
continuous shade

~

night takes the garden into itself

~

                    no hurry, says this man
with each rise of the fabric
leafed branch

~

shoulder aches
as if pain
meanders somewhere

~

                    to hold oneself in the palm
                    leather belt

~

small cages reincarnate to large
terrifying spaces where among others dark
black birds

~

beak of angel   winged sex

~

"fire over the lake"
to me desire is there

~

next time: always angling away
before assembling dream

                                        into coherence makes hay
                                        of the moment you left

~

likewise the corpses
small torment
along the lady banks rose
perfectly
still, yearning still

~

like blood, the little
tonsils of my fear
slide up & down

~

                                        wristwatch unclasped on its back

~

out of nowhere
bloom of catalpa
furrows in the neck's skin

~

                                        nipple of memory
press of roundness & earth

~

out of which worlds tumble
into afterlives
composed of anything

~

composed of slides, whorls
the rapt expressions of trunk & bark
face of stone

~

composed of root
circling back to
ochre streaks
blue line
which is not a river
which is not miraculous song

1
Of weakly allowing things to slide & drift along
as tomatoes deepen & turn
in the etched bowl, the one
abject place a dark scuzziness in the hole
tinged as she flips the omelette
or waiting with his hat still on
at the table

2
Perhaps a higher acting is concealed
in culinary fog
the white spatula's unremorseful
biography or the life of
forks, poised, empty, his,
hers, what enters the mouth, the cream
of possibility & eggs. The storm

3
Of a pitcher, this is the appearance of a bowl
& so the storm of a bowl

4
When one thing confronts us in the appearance
like he is eyeing her, saying so? & she is saying
so? & he

5
Goes beyond the appearance of objects
so far as to be frightening (to her), some
frightening beauty in his face, grazing—
as in a field

6
What is in question is the region

7
"A" region in which everything returns to itself
the dream of like-mindedness or rather
a fantasy of this photograph
the upside down world

with its roots & foundations
precisely reflecting what she thought to be true
then discovered

8
That we look into the horizon,
into the web of a face as if looking
would reveal it
smothered lock of eye
dull cheek
the tremor & the closed

9
Horizon is the openness which surrounds us
as now, shoveling food from the white
plate, believing sorrow to be
endemic, those two solitary motions

10
Because a word does not & never can re-present anything
&

11
Presumably we all become more waitful on our path
which is the path, necessarily,
we are on! (Horizon split like toast, jam
on his lips, her wrist) so that

12
A conversation on a country path
on a country path
about thinking
where tree branches
disclose triangular chinks of sky
& bird &
the river, as she recalls is,
is dark brown,
its foamy lip
creased, astonished

13
Which guided us deep into the night

setting
(The grazing curtain full of swans crossing the lake
   loop of primal longing
   odiferous feast in the wand-ish grass or an idea burrowing
   with better wings)

Thus us
as we appear to languish at the table,
smoking cigarettes & eating big red plates of pasta,
the sum of our forks making *tin-tin-tin* in the spaceful peace
& so echos

a dream of tonic scales recalled in *medias res*:
   —so then she stopped speaking to me
   —altogether?
   —jute-colored, soft—
   —her heart must be broken
   —a pair of wings, I mean

a chandelier with fourteen tear shaped bulbs, mosquitoed filaments,
   gorgeous in captivity—
a froth of crystal in whose prismed shards twirl excavations from the past—

(Dig Deeper, Freud advised, his mouth already full of depths and now the train—

like music—

       —no *exactly* music
       —I thought you'd say that—we've come all this way only to find ourselves
         afloat still, white feathered with
                            a history of cruelty
& now the walls, not white, but a sort of golden wash—
likewise her hair on her forehead & see
   the bowl of turnips flowing dimly in the candle fingers—
the chandelier you mean—
of crushed glass under a bleeding foot—
that time in the kitchen—
such bitter roots aswirl the mouth's dull cave—

Her heart was broken, we had to filch it up and dry it on some rock—
she never knew what hit her—

what swannish modes betake us, fat with conversation
the plastic drummer on his side beneath the one-legged table (covered
with embroidered cloth & fringed)
the plastic drummer, white-faced, absorbed,
a hat of red and black, looks straight ahead—
To what?
Her ruined heart, wrinkling in the sun—
I never knew her well—

what night was that?
Blank as tears, the night folded in on itself
its feet worn out from running
What did she wear?
A destiny of cotton
lace beneath her chin & foolish hopes
Was it this tonight?
Flat as paper until the wind came
& who else attends?
A cluster of arms plopped on the guard rail
crumpled napkin, smeared spoon
part of *of* a merest if

The world, he says pompously, can be found elsewhere, ample gesture of
his paw, otherwise. In velvet redder than a beet exhales a fringe of disbe-
lief: the world cannot be found at all. A silver fork upraised (& pointing
rudely) the other one intones the following:
    The world, why do we discuss her? She is at once here and not-here, her
    heart is cold, her feet covered with dirt and, how you say, garbage from
    the market—
Now a small gray woman who has kept her counsel taps a glass: Hush,
    hush, hush. Listen to the particular sound racing toward us—
—it's just the train

custard in whose depths a coin is buried
someone opened the window
the bleak night stood still there
as expected nothing came forward

About the Author

Karen Brennan is Professor in the Graduate Creative Writing Program at the University of Utah, and is also on the faculty of the Warren Wilson Program for Writers, She is the author of a book of poems, *Here on Earth* (Wesleyan, 1988), a memoir, *Being With Rachel* (Norton, 2002), and two collections of short fiction, *Wild Desire* (University of Massachusetts Press, 1991), and *The Garden in Which I Walk* (FC2, 2004). She has received the AWP Award in Fiction and a National Endowment for the Arts Fellowship.